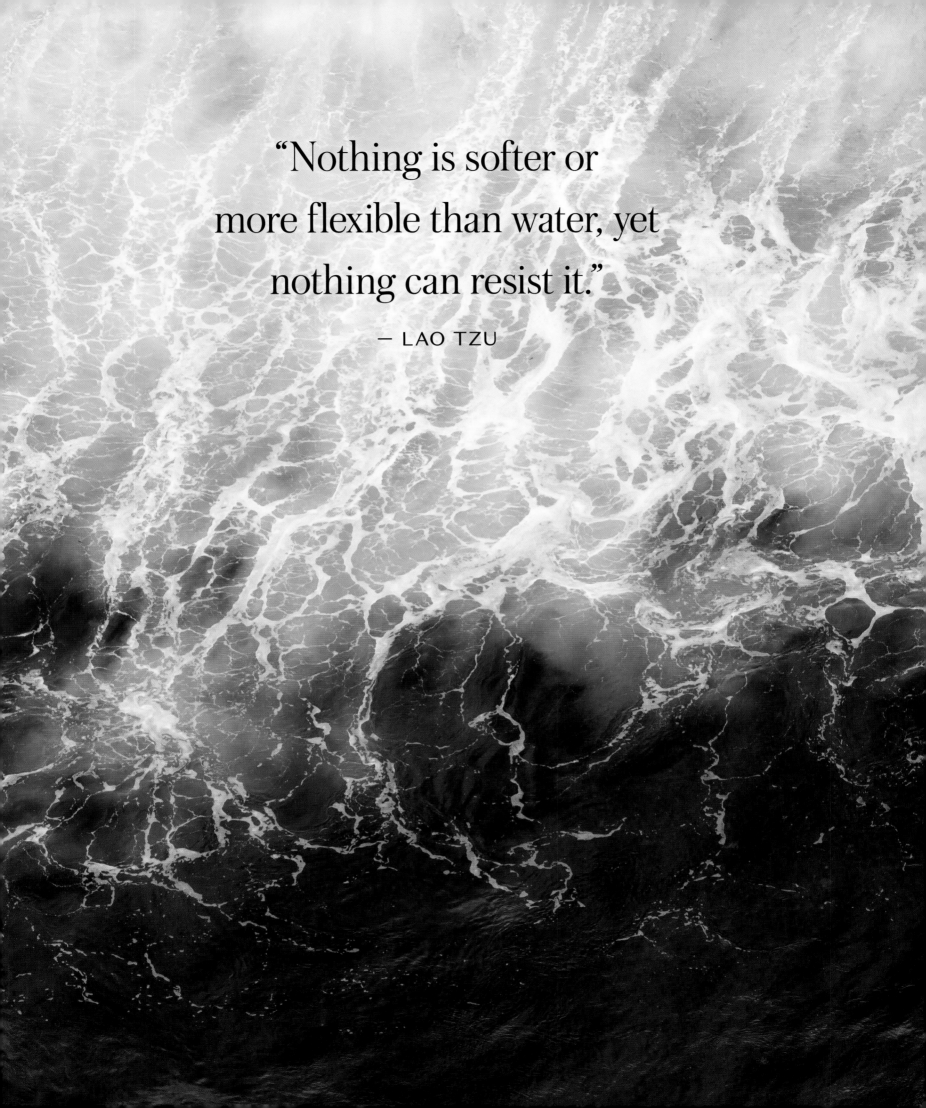

"Nothing is softer or
more flexible than water, yet
nothing can resist it."

— LAO TZU

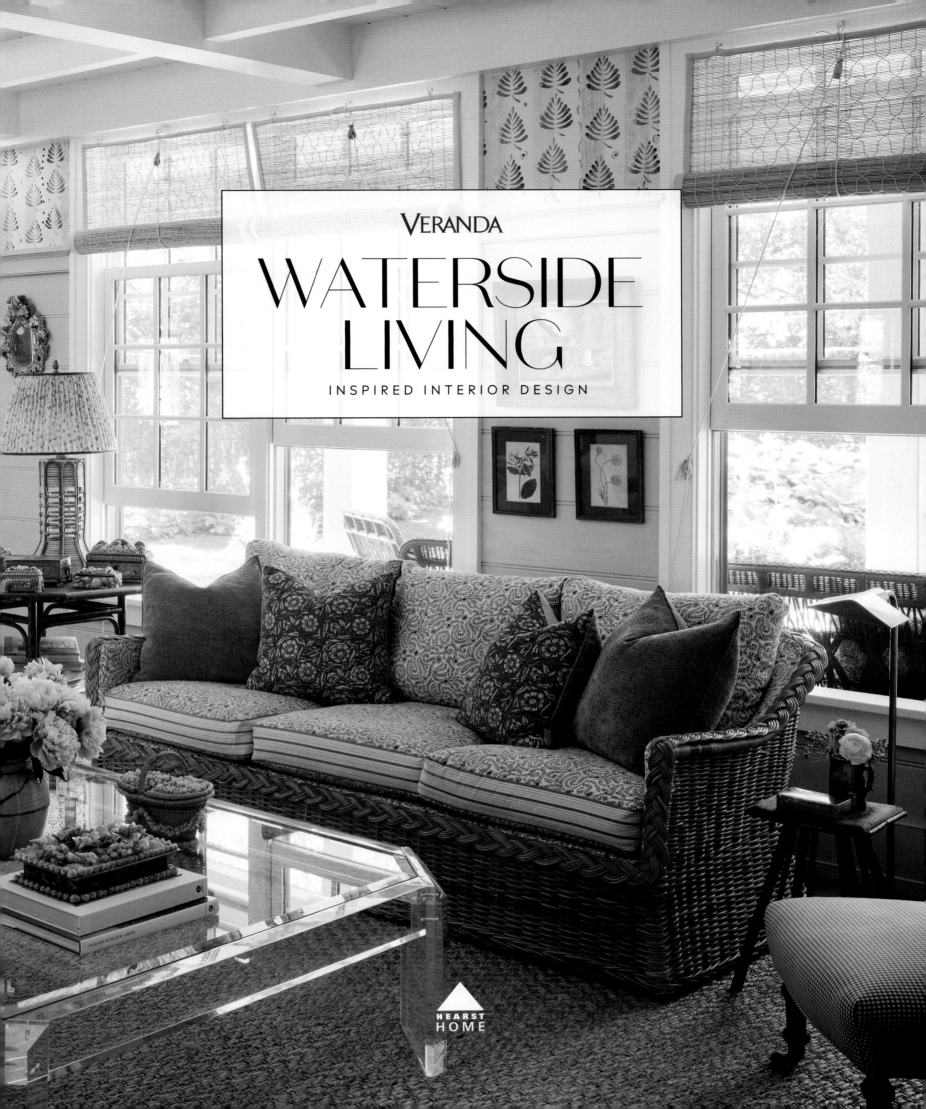

VERANDA
WATERSIDE LIVING
INSPIRED INTERIOR DESIGN

HEARST
HOME

contents

LEFT Teak, a material frequently used in nautical design, accents the cockpit of a yacht designed by Ken Fulk. Cushions covered in a zigzag-patterned outdoor fabric provide perches from which to survey the aquatic landscape.

PAGES 2-3 In the Nantucket home of Veronica Swanson Beard, the addition of a stylish acrylic table modernizes antique furniture and traditional floral fabrics. Swanson Beard's collection of shellwork boxes brings the home's coastal setting indoors.

foreword

"WE ARE TIED TO THE OCEAN. And when we go back to the sea—whether it is to sail or to watch it—we are going back from whence we came." President John F. Kennedy aptly described our enchantment with the water in remarks delivered to the 1962 America's Cup sailing crews in Newport, Rhode Island. Perhaps our oceanic origins have something to do with why so many of us are drawn to not just the water, but also design suited for waterside living.

Whether by a beach, a lake, or a river, all waterside homes celebrate leisure and a laid-back, welcoming atmosphere that fosters true comfort and relaxation. They also salute their surroundings with a design sensibility rooted in the landscape, making them well suited for *Veranda*, which honors sense of place. Furthermore, we believe the best waterside homes exude an irresistible ease that forms the foundation for memory making. Whether it's the wicker furniture with worn cushions, the soothing view of sunlight dancing on the water, or even the jigsaw puzzle that stumps you every season, these homes are tradition-filled treasure boxes with a lure as powerful and predictable as the tides themselves.

If you live on the water or dream of doing so, you'll find plenty of design and decorating inspiration—from color palettes well suited to seaside light to comfortable, durable furnishings that can stand up to life near the coast—in the waterside homes featured on these pages. But as author Jennifer Boles writes in her introduction, these houses—like all *Veranda* homes—are ultimately beguiling expressions of their owners' personalities. No matter where you live, I hope this book inspires you to embrace that same true-to-you spirit.

STEELE THOMAS MARCOUX

RIGHT Inside an Alys Beach, Florida, house, an open-air atrium and mosaic-lined splash pool designed by Khoury Vogt Architects were inspired by ancient Roman architecture. Sleek beaded curtains add a contemporary touch.

introduction

LIKE THE GRAVITATIONAL PULL OF AN OCEAN TIDE, water has drawn people to live along its shores since presumably the beginning of time. Some are moved to put down roots near a lake or a river for their livelihoods, perhaps by engaging in fishing or seafaring. Others are enticed by a coastal environment's natural beauty, making their decision to live waterside primarily a lifestyle choice—and as this book will attest, an attractive one at that. For a primary residence or an escape from the everyday, a home situated by the water can be as blissful as the landscape around it.

Oceanside locales are prime destinations in part because the sun and surf foster a laid-back atmosphere. The aqueous views are of course a draw, with water as far as the eye can see. Beach houses, then, tend to be designed accordingly: casually furnished, geared to relaxation, and providing maximum exposure to the surroundings. A similar atmosphere prevails inside most lake and riverside homes, but because the landscape is different, the design frequently is too. Abodes situated along inland bodies of water—often with surrounding trees sheltering them from intense sunlight—embrace richer colors and cozier furnishings, creating a sense of warmth inside that otherwise comes naturally in bright waterside settings. But as you'll see in some of the homes featured in this book, there are always exceptions to any rule.

The look of waterside homes often mirrors local culture too. Americana, particularly antique maritime paintings and Windsor chairs, remains a popular choice of decor for Nantucket seaside homes, for example. But in Palm Beach, colorful, preppy floral fabrics and vintage 20th-century rattan furnishings are—and have long been—all the rage. And in the case of Richard Smith's English Channel home, a free-spirited mix of patterns and prints reflects not only British custom but also the homeowners' ebullient personalities. Generalities aside, waterside homes can be anything their owners and designers wish them to be. It might not be every day that one encounters a newly built Florida beach house influenced by ancient Rome, or even a yacht that houses guests in Hawaiian-styled luxury, but that's the kind of freedom inherent in a coastal lifestyle.

Whether it's classic American coastal style that strikes your fancy or the tranquil atmosphere of a Caribbean idyll, prepare to be taken on a magnificent voyage, courtesy of VERANDA magazine.

LEFT Designed by Mark D. Sikes, the breakfast room at Grey Gardens, a storied East Hampton estate, plays host to an array of blue furnishings, including rattan dining chairs, a wicker pedestal and urn, and a custom china hutch.

CHAPTER ONE

A Fresh Perspective

IN SOME WATERSIDE COMMUNITIES, classic decor like stripes and nautical themes is as much a local custom as clambakes on the beach or bonfires by the lake. These motifs are entrenched in tradition, but when designers employ them in a new way, the results can be as refreshing as crisp salty air.

Along the coast of Maine, summer homes are often understated—low-key interiors have long been the norm. In a Colonial Revival–style house on Mount Desert Island, designer Matthew Carter introduced a high-style polish with bold colors and modern wallcoverings surrounding more traditional and expected furnishings. "When the project is to reinterpret the very idea of a classic summer house, that's the kind of fun you can have," Carter explains.

Designer Suzanne Rheinstein and architect Gil Schafer took a similar freethinking approach when revamping a stately Southern California residence. Rheinstein refined the home's seaside setting by introducing polished finishes reflective of its elegant architecture, like a living room ceiling lacquered the color of glistening sand and wall paneling painted to resemble driftwood. But in a newly constructed guesthouse, the designers shifted sails, devising a barnlike structure that Schafer describes as having "a sense of rustic informality." At first glance, limewashed shiplap walls and a Dutch gambrel roof evoke old New England, but with Rheinstein's choice of pared-down furnishings and contemporary flourishes, the guesthouse feels modern and beachy in its simplicity.

In some cases, designers reenergize traditional decor by using classic pieces colorfully and en masse, as a vibrant drift of hot pink bougainvillea. Lifestyle designer Julia Amory revels in her love of traditional furnishings. "These things make me feel safe and cozy," she says. In her Southampton home, a splashy trove of floral chintzes and wicker furniture creates a lively yet time-honored setting for her young family. In Armory's Palm Beach residence, similar decorations, this time in the quintessential Palm Beach combination of pink and green, are equally enticing. No matter the coastal setting, everything old can be made to feel new again.

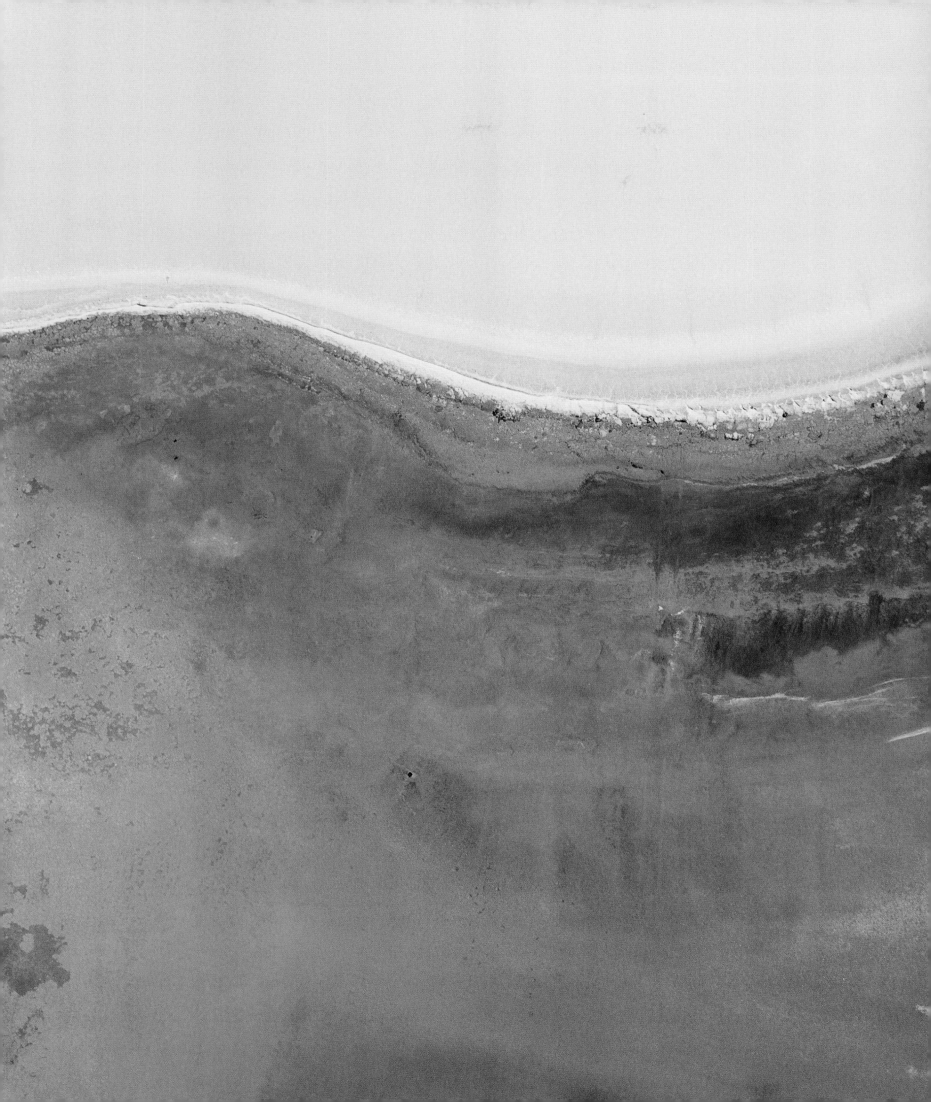

REFRESHING RETREAT

Matthew Carter recharges Down East tradition with all-American flair at a summer home in coastal Maine.

LEFT Most Maine summerhouses have a purposely undecorated feel, but Carter took a more polished approach that reflects his clients' Southern sensibilities. "The owners wanted to vamp up the house a bit. They have traditional tastes—arts, maps, antiques—but also a high threshold for color and pattern," Carter says. The entry hall's splashy Albert Hadley wallpaper, checkerboard-patterned floor, and zesty yellow stool are pleasingly high style.

RIGHT One of the home's more casual spaces, the vaulted glass breakfast room, feels relaxed and even a tad contemporary thanks to a stylish set of rattan chairs. The room's pale-green striped rug reflects the colors of Maine's forested coastline. "A home should nod to its place," Carter says.

LEFT Chocolate brown walls foster a dark, cool environment in the living room. The "deep color lets the walls recede and the windows expose the garden beyond," Carter says. A neutral sculpted rug provides a clean, modern foundation for the room's lively mix of antiques and traditional fabrics.

~~~~~~~~

ABOVE Carter's broad-minded approach to tradition
extends to the dining room. Classic decorations, including
an antique silver witches' ball and fern-print wallpaper
long associated with decorator Elsie de Wolfe, merge with
modern touches, such as a Noguchi paper globe lantern
and a gray ceiling.

BELOW Architecturally a "quintessential Maine summer house," according to the designer, the Colonial Revival–style home is steeped in tradition with its pea gravel driveway, green shutters, and crisp white porch, which is set for dining.

LEFT Carter felt that the study "needed depth, it needed punch, it needed something more than just paint," so he wrapped the space in patterned wallpaper, framing it with deep-green lacquer trim. The eclectic mix of seating includes a leafy-patterned wing chair and a modern rattan-wrapped desk chair.

LEFT Carter appoints the peaceful guest bedroom in a sea of soft blues that nod to the nearby Atlantic Ocean. Crisp striped fabrics, used on both the bench and the skirted chair, and subtle geometric-patterned wallpaper quietly enliven the space. A turquoise lamp provides a splash of saturated color.

RIGHT Botanical colors and details—light olive-green walls, a ceiling mobile that resembles leaves, and other natural accents such as a rattan cabinet and matchstick blinds—create a verdant atmosphere in the bathroom.

ABOVE Reminiscent of a tranquil garden, the primary bedroom channels the home's lush green landscape with its gingko-patterned wallpaper by Colefax and Fowler and green accents including embroidered bed linens and an upholstered chair and ottoman.

FAMILY TIES

Treasured heirlooms and timeless floral fabrics
make linen designer Julia Amory and her family feel
at home in both the Hamptons and Palm Beach.

PAGES 22-23 For her Palm Beach sitting room, Julia Amory indulged in the resort town's signature color, pink, detailing the ceiling in soft-pink cabana stripes, papering walls in conch-shell pink grass cloth, and staining the floor pale pink. "We're not trying to rewrite the history of Palm Beach here," Amory says.

ABOVE Amory is unabashed in her enthusiasm for floral chintz fabrics, especially Colefax and Fowler's Fuchsia. She uses the blue version for upholstery and window shades in her Southampton library, seen here, and the pink variation in her Palm Beach living room. "Some people go crazy about not repeating motifs, but I like the cohesion it gives," Amory says.

RIGHT The serving pantry in the Palm Beach home is charming and nostalgic thanks to trellis-print wallpaper highlighted by aqua-colored cabinetry and trim.

ABOVE A birdcage chandelier is one of the Palm Beach dining room's many details, which also include floral-patterned linen voile slipcovers and a geometric-patterned floor. Braided grass-cloth wallpaper and a rattan urn and column strike a beachy note.

LEFT A Palm Beach bathroom's unlikely combination of gingham sink skirting, zinc lanterns, and a Renaissance-inspired, floral-patterned wallpaper reflects Amory's carefree way of combining traditional elements. "These houses aren't decorating projects," she says. "This is just how we live."

LEFT Fearless when it comes to mixing patterns, Amory assembled pink-checkered wallpaper and fabric, a floral chintz headboard and bed curtains, and heart-strewn bed linens in a Palm Beach bedroom. Used together, the traditional prints appear bold and vivacious.

RIGHT On the Southampton porch, green-and-white-striped cushions and a bevy of floral-print pillows dress the classic bottle-green wicker seating. "Green is basically a neutral for me, and dark green is my black," Amory says. A profusion of hydrangeas appears throughout the property.

Wicker & Rattan

Among the most favored of classic design materials, wicker and rattan have long been synonymous with relaxed living. Widely popular during Victorian times, when wicker furniture could often be found indoors in winter garden rooms, hand-woven wicker and rattan pieces add a nostalgic and charming touch to any setting. Maybe that's why Sister Parish, the doyenne of traditional decorating, had such a fondness for them.

Similar to how Parish decorated with wicker furniture—usually with the accompaniment of floral chintz or striped fabrics—Julia Amory assembled new and vintage wicker pieces on the veranda of her Southampton home, where a set of dark green wicker sofas and chairs are lavished with both striped cushions and floral throw pillows. In fact, color is a major selling point of wicker and rattan—it can be painted any shade desired. For his clients' villa in Mustique, Veere Grenney chose classic white wicker furniture for the living room, enhancing its airiness (page 160). Quite the opposite are the bright-blue rattan chairs and wicker urns that accent the breakfast room at Grey Gardens, adding even more bursts of color to an already vibrant space (page 108).

Even though wicker furniture is traditional, it can still be modern. At the art-filled Vero Beach home of Ellen Hamilton's clients, a set of Franco Albini woven wicker lounge chairs, considered by many to be a midcentury work of art, stands out thanks to its curving, contemporary design (page 42). Inherently pliable, wicker and rattan can harmonize with any waterside setting.

~~~~~~~~~~

RIGHT As detailed as an interior space, the loggia in Julia Armory's Florida home is a hit parade of classic Palm Beach flourishes, including wicker, Chinese Chippendale–style chairs, a ceramic garden stool, and orchids ensconced in woven rattan baskets.

A WARM WELCOME

A Newport Beach property, revamped by
Suzanne Rheinstein and Gil Schafer, becomes a casually
elegant gathering spot for family and friends.

LEFT Built for entertaining, the guesthouse was intended to be casual. "We didn't want the new structure to upstage the main house," says architect Schafer. "We wanted a sense of rustic informality," evident in his choice of limewashed shiplap for the great room's walls, a nod to East Coast style.

RIGHT The great room's high-beamed ceiling gives it a barnlike feel. At the same time, Suzanne Rheinstein's sophisticated yet relaxed mix of furnishings, such as a weathered column and a pair of Napoleon III club chairs, elevates the tone of the space.

LEFT Modern flourishes, including contemporary art, oversize swing-arm lamps, and curvy rattan seating, contemporize the guesthouse's New England architecture.

A FRESH PERSPECTIVE   35

LEFT Vivid blue cabinetry—the hue of the nearby sea—enlivens a small, well-stocked kitchen in the guesthouse.

RIGHT Rheinstein uses warm, sandy tones for the main house's living room, whose crowning touch is a shimmering lacquered ceiling that reflects sunlight. A lack of floor coverings takes the room's formality down a notch.

ABOVE The main house's family room is awash in watery hues. A laid-back, neutral-colored striped sofa and a coffee table laden with books create an ideal environment for easy living.

"Newport Beach is studded with
Colonial Revival houses . . .
that call to mind a kind of California
fantasy of East Coast living."

—ARCHITECT GIL SCHAFER

ABOVE Enveloped in a verdant shade of spring green, a bedroom in the main house beckons guests with its fairy-tale-like canopy bed. Rheinstein selected an exuberant floral-print fabric by Raoul Textiles for the headboard, canopy, and bedding.

RIGHT A guest bedroom, situated under an eave of the guesthouse's Dutch gambrel roof, is soothing and warm with a soft color palette. The lavish use of embroidered floral fabric engulfs the walls, ceiling, and bed. "Those quirky spaces upstairs are cozy and intimate," Schafer says.

CHAPTER TWO

Vibrant Expressions

WHETHER ACCENTED IN TROPICAL SHADES reflective of sultry locales or blanketed in cozy colors and prints to generate interior warmth, waterside homes bedecked in bold hues and patterns dazzle as kaleidoscopically as a colorful cache of seashells.

Some designers, like Ellen Hamilton, are fearless when it comes to colors and patterns. Inspired by her clients' high-octane art collection, Hamilton took an adventurous tack when designing a spacious Vero Beach house. Bold strokes of color, such as chartreuse walls and hot-pink outdoor furniture, and vigorously patterned fabrics and finishes complement the knockout contemporary art inside and outside the house—including poolside. "The Florida light is so different from anywhere else; it begs to have high-impact art and color," the homeowner says.

Designer Summer Thornton, also a color and pattern enthusiast, uses both to revitalize a languishing early-1920s inn on the shore of Lake Michigan. Captivated by the property's wooded setting, she instilled what she calls an "alpine fairy-tale feel" into each room, lavishing them with patterned mash-ups that include colorful checks, stripes, and floral prints. "There isn't the openness and brightness of a beach house. Rather, it's eclectic with potential for a little country fantasy or even a quirky English cottage," Thornton says.

For Richard Smith, purchasing a 17th-century house on a bluff overlooking the English Channel gave the British fabric designer a chance to experiment with his vibrant textile designs. "I made the most of the opportunity to get a better sense of how the fabrics perform in real life," Smith says. His design alchemy, a free-spirited mix of patterns and colors, enlivens every room of the house, especially his bedroom, where a black-striped fabric is paired with a patterned wallpaper inspired by a Japanese screen. Brimming with a charming eccentricity that is thoroughly British, the home speaks to the best aspects of coastal living.

ART APPRECIATION

Ellen Hamilton turns a Florida home into a one-of-a-kind masterpiece, inside and out, making the most of electrifying color and a collection of contemporary art.

PAGE 42 A 10-by-70-foot ceramic and lava-stone tile mural created by artist Michelle Grabner is a dynamic backdrop for the pool at this Vero Beach home. "We wanted something to animate the space," says the homeowner, who hired Ellen Hamilton to design the home's equally vibrant interiors.

PAGE 43 A high-impact painting by L.A. artist Whitney Bedford is the focus of the home's entry, creating an energetic welcome that delights the homeowner. "It's got incredible punch and interest. I kind of love that it's the first thing you see when you come in," the owner says. A Paul Mathieu floor lamp stands tall nearby.

LEFT A work of art in its own right, the kitchen features walls lined in braid-patterned glazed tiles by Fornace Brioni. Yellow-and-black bar stools play off the walls' coloration.

ABOVE A pair of striking Cubist glass-topped tables and steel chairs covered in a houndstooth fabric fill the kitchen's breakfast nook with personality. A Pop Art piece by Hassan Hajjaj bookends the space.

RIGHT Jolts of orange, painted stools, and a bindis mirror by artist Bharti Kher bring the living room to life. "We buy pieces that move us, and then it's fun to figure out how it all works together," says the homeowner, an avid art collector.

LEFT The covered porch is an ideal spot to dine, particularly given its location next to the pool. Rattan chairs offer cool comfort in the sweltering heat.

RIGHT Blush-toned draperies help filter sunlight streaming into the second-floor porch, where a set of woven spherical lounge chairs by Janus et Cie and white slipcovered sofas provide seating. The indoor-outdoor flow of the house is "very porous," says the home's architect, Hope Dana.

"The art is such a self-expression of my client, our muse. It's only fitting that the design mirrors that simultaneous expression."

—DESIGNER ELLEN HAMILTON

LEFT The sitting room is a patchwork of color and pattern, including Pop Art portraits by artist Hassan Hajjaj and a sectional covered in a bamboo-leaf print fabric. The homeowner selected the art pieces because she knew they would come alive in Florida's light. "It begs to have high-impact art and color," the owner says.

ABOVE One of the most important pieces in the homeowners' collection, a collage by Rashid Johnson, hangs with pride in the dining room. A chartreuse wall and brass cube sconces frame the work.

LEFT A dynamic marbled clay tile floor adds a touch of delight in the owners' bathroom, where an oil and charcoal painting by Magnus Plessen is displayed above the bathtub.

LEFT Hamilton works with mostly green furnishings for the guest room, such as a pair of custom glass-paneled wardrobes that are embellished with patterned laminated wallpaper by Gucci. The homeowner describes the wardrobes as "Ellen pushing the envelope. Instead of traditional closets, she said, 'Let's do something cool.'"

RIGHT Aqua walls and accents, plus a graphic-patterned fireplace surround, create a robust atmosphere. Terrazzo floors, intended as a nod to the homeowners' Italian heritage, appear inside the house and continue into this outdoor space, connecting both environments.

HAIL BRITANNIA

Textile designer Richard Smith's 17th-century house, perched above the English Channel, towers with robust personality.

LEFT For the entry of Fairlight Place, his home overlooking the English Channel, designer Richard Smith introduced something unexpected: a black-and-white-striped Victorian tented wardrobe that reflects the home's insouciant spirit. "Fairlight Place is a handsome and unpretentious manor house happy in its own skin," Smith says.

RIGHT The home's large drawing room, situated in the oldest part of the house, which dates to the 17th century, did not pose a challenge to the homeowner. Instead, Smith employed designs produced by his textile company, Madeaux. "To unify the two halves, I covered both in the same shell-pink wallcovering and repeated fabrics on the windows and settees."

RIGHT On this side of the drawing room, lively fabrics, including a robust fern print used for curtains and a flame-stitch fabric that covers the settee, blanket the space in patterned warmth. The inglenook hearth also proves useful on chilly days.

LEFT Smith and his partner, Andrew Blackman, enjoy entertaining outdoors. "Friends coming for dinner know to bring several layers as they will most likely be made to sit outside in anything even approaching good weather," he says. The outdoor dining area overlooks the home's expansive grounds.

RIGHT In one of the bathrooms, a claw-foot tub, surrounded by a charming bamboo trellis wallpaper, faces the English Channel.

"I have come to rely on the house as an invaluable design laboratory."

—HOMEOWNER AND DESIGNER RICHARD SMITH

LEFT "Two themes repeat throughout the house: black and stripes," says Smith, who credits a Japanese screen with inspiring the black-background bird and botanical print that animates the walls, bed cover, and canopy in his bedroom. A charcoal-striped linen-silk fabric adorns the headboard, bed hangings, and lampshade.

LEFT Smith is particularly fond of sepia tones, featured here in the floral pattern used on walls and upholstery: "I've always loved the palette's simple beauty." He added the red drapery pelmets for "a bit of humor."

Stripes

Given their nautical association, stripes have long been a go-to pattern in coastal environments, embraced by seafarers and land lovers alike. None other than Coco Chanel made the classic striped Breton pullover a wardrobe staple, universalizing a look that had been worn by French navy sailors. By the turn of the 20th century, stripes had become a popular waterside flourish on any number of furnishings, from beach tents used for changing clothes to deck chairs on passenger ships, a tradition that continues today.

At Grey Gardens, Mark D. Sikes, a well-known fan of the pattern, chose stripes in blue and white for a set of canopied chaise longues that feel very French Riviera (page 116). He also had the walls and ceiling of a nearby cabana painted exclusively with stripes, giving it the impression of a tent—a decorative effect also used by Richard Smith in this dining room to create a festive atmosphere for his dinner parties.

Even when they're not the main attraction, stripes still have a way of commanding attention. At a Lake Michigan inn designed by Summer Thornton, snappy red-and-white-striped umbrellas accent its outdoor spaces (page 66). Indoors, red-and-white curtains, thinly striped, create a peppermint-stick effect around the lounge's windows (pages 70-71). And what some stripes may lack in color, they more than make up for in quiet elegance, as seen in the subtle upholstery that Suzanne Rheinstein selected for her clients' gracious Newport Beach home (page 32).

LEFT The kitchen houses an eclectic mix of patterns, including a French patchwork wallcovering that Smith says he designed "to bring a warm, fun atmosphere to what is probably our most-used room."

ABOVE The dining room is made for entertaining thanks to its striped ceiling, trim, and corner poles, which create a tentlike effect. "It's more flamboyant than our usual style, but it certainly gives our dinner parties a sense of occasion," Smith says.

PATTERN PLAY

Designer Summer Thornton brings whimsy
and fun to a once-sleepy inn on Lake Michigan.

ABOVE Red-striped umbrellas and a Dutch door painted in Farrow & Ball's Brinjal are the first indications that this former Lake Michigan inn has embarked on a colorful new chapter. Now used as a private retreat for the owners and their guests, the inn maintains a ground-floor restaurant that is open to the public.

RIGHT Designer Summer Thornton plied the interior spaces with whimsy and eclecticism, starting with the entry hall's antique Swedish Mora clock, old-fashioned floral rug, and burgundy-striped table skirt. "There's a sense of nostalgia in this house, but there is also the unanticipated," she says.

LEFT Classic woven café chairs and an antique barley-twist chair, which echo the entry hall's burgundy-and-red color scheme, hold court in the restaurant. An exuberant botanical print wallcovering by House of Hackney and an abstract patterned ceiling paper add some spice to the space.

RIGHT Thornton used different colorways of the same checked fabric—Jim Thompson's Square Dance—for bar stools in the restaurant bar. The large checkerboard floor adds another dimension to the lively space.

LEFT Thornton furnished many rooms with antiques, including the Empire chest seen here. "It was so important that this house feel collected and authentic, like you've just been adding things in over the years from different places."

PAGES 70-71 The upstairs lounge is bursting with colorful pattern. A checkerboard sofa, red-and-white-striped curtains, and floral-strewn wallpaper are joined by an unusual black Bessarabian kilim rug. "I knew I wanted this particular kind of rug—it's busy and lively and can take a lot of wear and tear," Thornton says.

LEFT A subtle diamond-print wallpaper by Robert Kime balances a guest room's bolder elements, such as a striped headboard, floral curtains, and a marigold-hued blanket. A painting of a ship by Connecticut artist Mary Maguire draws the inn's waterside setting inside.

LEFT The designer embellished many of the home's upholstered chairs with skirts because they "give a sense of groundedness and are obviously more old-fashioned." A floral print wallpaper also feels nostalgic.

RIGHT This guest bathroom is appointed in fixtures and finishes that embrace the inn's 1920s roots, such as a chrome-legged sink and a classic hexagon-patterned tile floor. Each bathroom features a woodland-style mirror.

LEFT For the owner's suite, Thornton worked with a soft green and cream palette, giving the room a cozy and serene feel. The bed is upholstered in a Holly Hunt checked fabric.

RIGHT Thornton commissioned Maguire to produce artwork throughout the inn, including these charming ship paintings on display in the upper lounge wet bar. Faux-bois wallpaper provides a naturalistic backdrop for them.

"There are the usual suspects in summer homes such as wicker, bamboo, rattan, and old painted pieces like trunks and tables, but all thrown together in a very whimsical and colorful way."

—DESIGNER SUMMER THORNTON

CHAPTER THREE

New Directions

MINIMALIST, GLASSY, ORGANIC, or sometimes rough-hewn, modern coastal style takes shape in any number of striking ways. Even in a design landscape rich with possibility, some modern coastal homes find distinctive and surprising ways to express themselves.

In the case of a newly built vacation house in Alys Beach, Florida, it was a desire to be surrounded by water that led to a bold idea. The homeowners said that they wished for "water, water, everywhere," so the home's architects, Marieanne Khoury-Vogt and Erik Vogt, responded adventurously. They introduced an ancient Roman concept into the heart of the house: an open-air atrium with a shallow, mosaic-lined pool integrated into the floor. Inspired by antiquity but hardly antiquated, the atrium—and the rest of the house—feels innovative and exciting thanks to the sleek architecture surrounding it and designer Shirlene Brooks's understated interior design.

For a Connecticut lake house nestled in the woods, it was the ingenuity of designer David Kleinberg and architect Tom Kligerman that sparked the home's special look. On the outside, the home exudes traditional lakeside style with dark wood siding and a cabin-like appearance meant to harmonize with its natural surroundings. Step through the front door, and you'll be delighted by unexpected twists, such as an entry-hall library boasting floor-to-ceiling views of the lake. "It's a surprising way to walk into a house," Kleinberg says.

Even design elements frequently seen in modern coastal homes, such as a light color palette, can be trailblazing when venturing where least expected. In a clients' Costa Rican getaway, designer Beth Webb lavished the interiors in soft neutral hues, including creamy fabrics, pale walls, and bleached wood cabinetry, a divergence from the dark wood typically found in homes in the area. "People can equate neutral with boring," says Webb, who achieved the opposite by introducing layers of texture to give the color palette richness. In fact, given the creativity that seems to be stoked when designing a house by the water, excitement is practically guaranteed.

MODERN CLASSIC

Khoury Vogt Architects and designer Shirlene Brooks take inspiration from ancient Roman architecture and create a truly original Alys Beach home.

LEFT The homeowners wanted to be surrounded by water and to "replicate the way it relaxes you both physically and mentally." Architects Marieanne Khoury-Vogt and Eric Vogt designed this Florida home around an open-air central atrium with a splash pool, an idea inspired by ancient Roman architecture. The atrium's linen-colored stucco walls reflect the home's Mediterranean influence.

RIGHT Even with its strong classical influence the home's architecture also feels contemporary, particularly in the understated primary bedroom, which opens onto an open-air courtyard that blurs the line between indoors and outdoors. Accordion bifold doors let the owners close off the space as they wish.

LEFT Brooks established an ultra-quiet palette in the living room, where curtains and linen sofas in a mix of creams, naturals, and white foster a sense of tranquility. There are accents of deep blue, which the designer chose because they "mirror the Gulf," and the Tyrrhenian Sea of the Mediterranean—an inspiration for the home's architecture.

RIGHT The bar, adjacent to the rooftop pool, has a playful feel with jazzy aquatic blue-glazed Moroccan tile.

"The architecture of this home speaks volumes, so I felt like everything else needed to whisper."

—DESIGNER SHIRLENE BROOKS

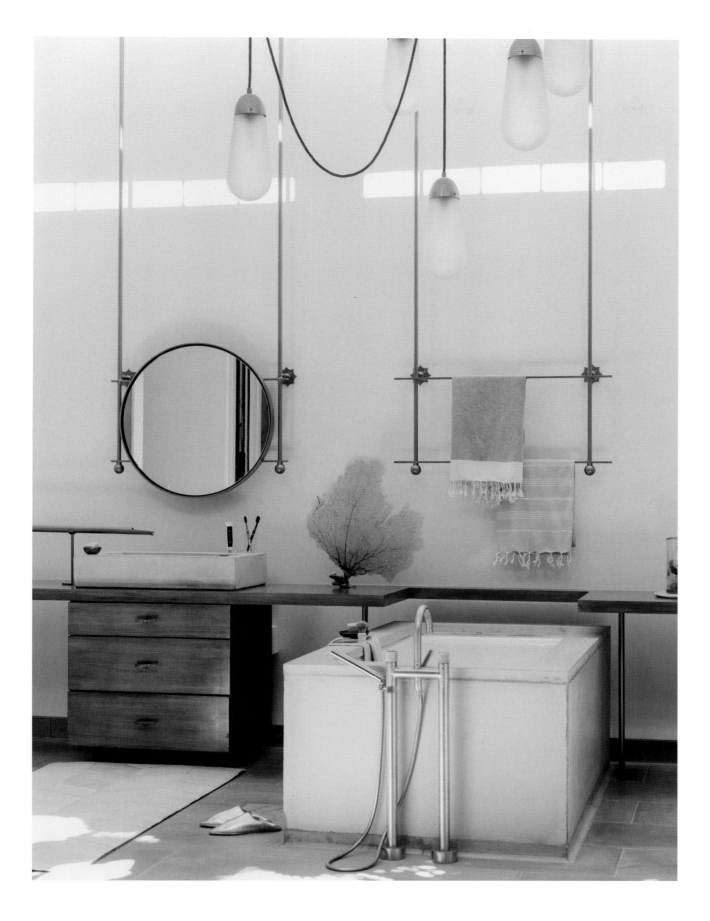

LEFT A suspended light fixture by Apparatus, joined by a sleek mirror and towel rack, adds drama to the otherwise serene primary bathroom.

LEFT Just like the rest of the house, the primary bedroom is rich in architectural details, including a spectacular decorative window above a sculpted bed that ushers in additional light.

THE FINISHING TOUCH
Pools

Whether a sybaritic indulgence or a recreational necessity, swimming pools have become a familiar presence at coastal abodes, providing swimmers and sunbathers alike with the opportunity to relax or cool off in the privacy of one's home. Much like the architecturally elaborate versions built by the ancient Greeks and Romans—some of the earliest advocates of swimming pools—today's pools are as meticulously designed as the houses they accompany.

Many pools reflect the prevailing aesthetic of a residence, like the one located at the Vero Beach estate designed by Ellen Hamilton (page 42). Treated as artistically and colorfully as the house itself, a massive abstract glazed-tile mural flanks the home's pool. Another outdoor masterpiece is the rim overflow rooftop pool conceived by architects Khoury Vogt, which offers the homeowners and their guests the sensation of swimming in the sky.

Sometimes the showstopping feature is the pool's location. When outfitting the pool area at his West Palm Beach home, Lou Marotta took a less-is-more approach. Surrounded by layers of lush, tropical landscaping—an ideal setting for a pool, some might say—the verdant oasis is outfitted simply but enticingly, with two teak lounge chairs on one side and a pair of antique French carved-stone figures on the other (page 218). So whether splashy or toned down, a pool is always a refreshing addition, no matter its design.

ABOVE A rim overflow rooftop pool appears to wash over the surrounding residences of Alys Beach.

BELOW A shallow pool, surrounded by beaded steel curtains for added flair, is the atrium's centerpiece. "It catches the rainwater and facilitates air circulation. So it essentially becomes the lungs of the house, along with a really beautiful social center for the family," Khoury-Vogt says. An underwater mosaic of dancing fish is another nod to ancient Rome.

DUAL NATURE

Designer David Kleinberg and architect Tom Kligerman
compose a naturalist's paradise in a Connecticut lake house
with splashes of red, blue, and woodland ingenuity.

LEFT The kitchen shines with a palette of lightly colored materials, such as glazed white tile, Carrara marble, and pale oak, serving as a foil to the home's dark exterior. Soft blue cabinetry adds a subtle aquatic note to the space.

RIGHT Midcentury furniture, especially Scandinavian pieces, appears throughout the house, including in the breakfast nook, where steel-and-leather stools surround a 1940s Swedish table. "We focused on a period when designers were taking existing forms and cleaning them up in a slightly more modern way," says designer Terrence Charles, who worked with Kleinberg.

PAGES 88-89 The homeowners refer to their Connecticut lake retreat, which was fashioned by designer David Kleinberg and architect Tom Kligerman, as "the tree house" because of its wooded setting, which creates a stunning panorama surrounding the home's enclosed porch. A set of Bielecky rattan chairs and vibrant blue tables enhance the landscape.

LEFT The homeowners wished for the house to be "understated and easy and tailored and collected," so the designers introduced unfussy yet sophisticated furnishings not often seen in lakehouses, such as the 1970s Danish chairs and a 1940s-era French cocktail table that adorn the living room.

LEFT One of the home's most distinctive spaces is its entry hall, which doubles as a library. Upon walking through the barn-red Dutch door, one is greeted by views of the water in the picture windows opposite the doorway. "There's a feeling of anticipation as you look through floor-to-ceiling windows out at the lake," Kleinberg says.

ABOVE Rich colors, used judiciously, are a hallmark of the house. Here, in a guest bedroom, windows are trimmed in ruby paint.

LIGHT AND BREEZY

Designer Beth Webb's trademark subtle neutral hues
plus tropical regional influences set the tone
for carefree elegance in this Costa Rican getaway.

LEFT Taking inspiration from Mediterranean and Central American styles, architect Lew Oliver designed this Costa Rican family getaway as an H-shaped house with loggias on both floors, fostering seamless indoor-outdoor living. "It seems like a significant estate, but our house is on a modest piece of land that we use intensely," the homeowner says.

RIGHT The home's fountain and loggia, where the owners enjoy spending their evenings, are tiled in Coralina stone pavers, a material frequently used in tropical environments because of its low heat retention. Sun-filtering sheer curtains and climbing ivy also help lower the temperature inside the space.

RIGHT Designer Beth Webb enriched the living room's neutral color palette with a textured woven rug and patterned curtains that filter the tropical sunlight. "It's how you mix the quietness of the color with the surrounding textures that excites me," Webb says. An antique suzani throw, draped over the sofa's back, also animates the space.

ABOVE The kitchen dining area's contrasting white-and-brown floor tile was designed by the homeowner and made in Costa Rica, where the owner says true espresso brown tile is hard to come by. "Everything has an orange cast. Thankfully, they were able to take the fire out of it."

RIGHT In lieu of the dark wood often found in Costa Rican houses, the kitchen island has a soft ceruse finish that ties together the space's creamy plaster walls and patterned-tile backsplash.

LEFT To prevent the house from being too "casa Americana," Webb and her client sourced many of the home's materials and furnishings in Mexico City, including folk art–like bed linens by textile designer Maggie Galton.

RIGHT In the primary bathroom, a soaking tub faces the window—and lush outdoor views. The glossy pebbled flooring is reminiscent of the beach.

CHAPTER FOUR

True Blue

BLUE: A COLOR THAT SPANS THE DARK, INKY TONES found deep within the ocean to the airy, atmospheric shades of the sky. It's associated with relaxation, calmness, and serenity, so it's no surprise, then, that designers draw inspiration and employ many shades of the color throughout waterside homes.

Designer Kelli Ford lavished the interior of her Hamptons summer retreat in watery blue hues, allowing her and her family to revel in the beauty of the surrounding ocean and bay, even while indoors. Ford and her design partner sister, who proclaim themselves "mad for blue, white, and pattern," left in place the inherited tile finishes from the previous owner—including an enticing array of blue-and-white tilework in the living room and kitchen. They then maximized the sensation of being by the water by introducing even more blue and white in the form of patterned fabrics.

For some, blue helps foster a relaxed, casual atmosphere. But for others, like fashion designer Liz Lange, the color is used to supercharge a home's interiors with bold personality. While restoring the famed East Hampton estate Grey Gardens, Lange (with the aid of designers Jonathan Adler and Mark D. Sikes) imbued some of the home's living spaces with a colorful 1960s and '70s vibe not often seen on the East Coast. Blue leopard-print wallpaper greets guests in the home's foyer, while a turquoise-colored floor and vibrant blue furniture are two of the many blue details that define the breakfast room. "This house definitely makes a statement," Lange says.

Best of all, blue is a universally flattering color, no matter a home's style or setting. When Sikes made over another client's home in Pacific Palisades, California, he melded his signature all-American look with traditional Provençal flair. Although the patterned tile, French-inspired fabrics, casual striped rugs, and even Chinese porcelains that Sikes assembled are stylistically diverse, he unified them by adhering to a crisp blue-and-white palette. The result is a house whose pulled-together yet eclectic interior is suitable for landlocked and waterside locales alike, including the Southern California coast. Indeed, blue has such versatility that when used indoors, the possibilities are as vast as the ocean.

A NEW BEGINNING

Bold choices by fashion entrepreneur Liz Lange
and designers Jonathan Adler and Mark D. Sikes revive
Grey Gardens, a storied East Hampton estate.

LEFT An offbeat mix of aqua furnishings, including leopard-print wallpaper, a skirted table, and the stair runner's trim, might seem surprising for Grey Gardens, one of East Hampton's grand old estates, but it captures the personality of the home's owner, fashion designer Liz Lange. "Liz has always embodied a true idiosyncratic style with swagger," says her friend Jonathan Adler, who designed some of the home's interiors, with designer Mark D. Sikes overseeing the rest.

RIGHT The house's restoration involved adding back period-appropriate details, such as diamond-paned windows with restoration glass, and overhauling the walled garden seen here. Blue shutters and striped awnings are fitting choices for a beach house.

RIGHT Sikes was responsible for the breakfast room, whose blue-hued furnishings include a set of Soane Britain rattan chairs painted in Farrow & Ball's Lulworth Blue. The floral wall covering and curtains reference the garden outside.

RIGHT Adler wrapped the dining room walls in deep teal silk, a rich backdrop for a display of porcelain depicting flowers that grow on the property. Chartreuse side chairs, an Adler design, add a bright twist to the room's predominantly watery hues.

ABOVE Blue is present in nearly every room in the house. The kitchen features a pale-blue floor surrounded by clean white marble and cabinetry.

LEFT On the second-story landing, a papier-mâché bust of "Little Edie" Bouvier surveys the scene from atop a bookcase. Made by Mark Gagnon, the sculpture is "a wink or nod to the former owners" of the house and one of Grey Gardens's most famous occupants, Lange says.

RIGHT Bennison's reverse toile, which graces an attic bedroom's walls, ceiling, window shades, and accent pillows, is traditional yet fresh with its saturated green hue. "The idea was to be respectful of the history and the house but make it reflective of who lives there today," Sikes says.

LEFT A pair of bright-blue upholstered Mastercraft chairs and a midcentury chandelier, seen in the living room, are two of the home's many vintage pieces. The sofa's fabric, Arbre de Matisse Reverse by Quadrille, is a nod to design great Billy Baldwin.

"There's almost a quietness and you feel like you don't even know where you are. It has this strangely magical, peaceful, beautiful atmosphere."

—FASHION ENTREPRENEUR LIZ LANGE

ABOVE A bedroom papered in a different Bennison floral print offers guests the opportunity to sleep among the flowers. Decorative painter Bob Christian repeated the print on crown molding and a four-poster bed.

RIGHT The attic game room is furnished unexpectedly with green-and-white-striped bean bag chairs. Although likely rarely found in traditional Hamptons houses, the quirky chairs are emblematic of Lange's adventurous spirit. "To me, taste should be kind of controversial," Lange says. The leafy stripe wallpaper is by Soane Britain.

RIGHT Patterned after the Beverly Hills home of legendary film producer Robert Evans, the round pool is made to look even more glamorous with a trellised gazebo and Munder Skiles lounge chairs designed by Sikes.

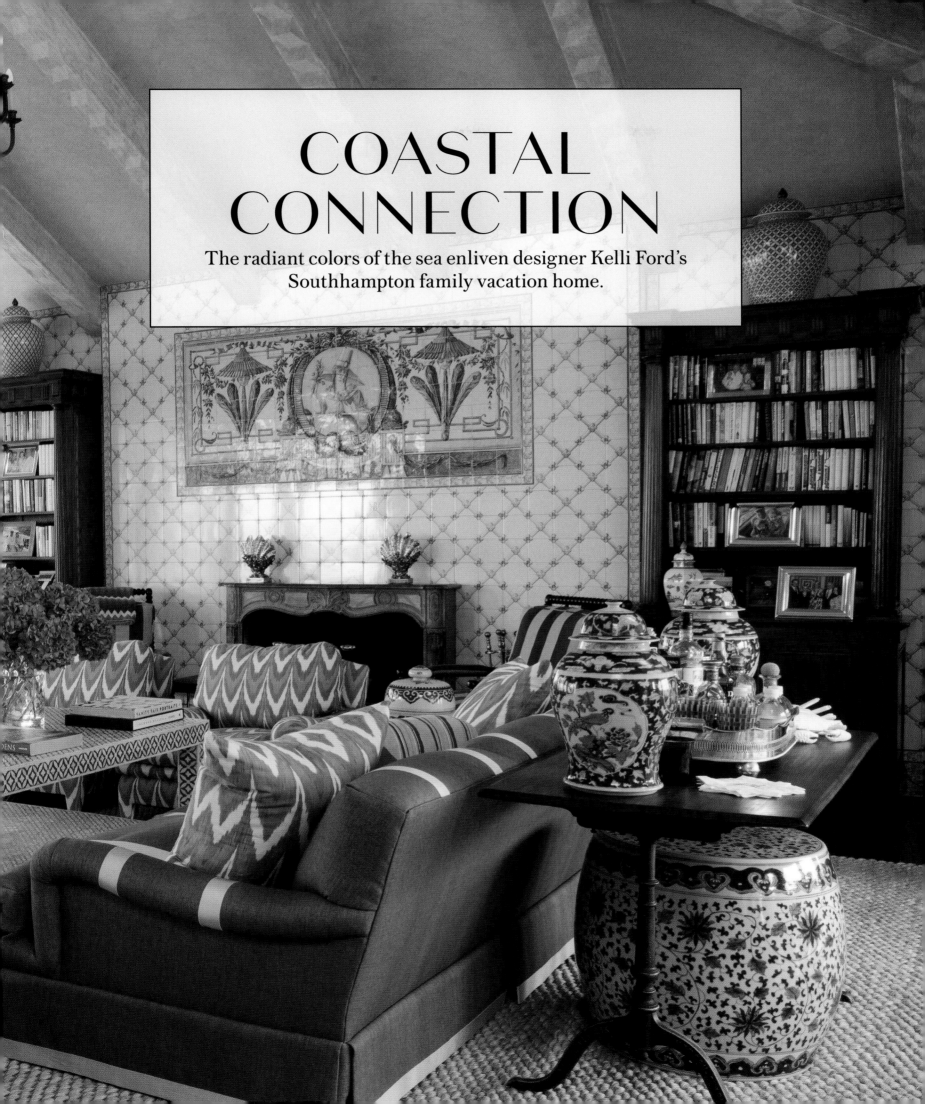

COASTAL CONNECTION

The radiant colors of the sea enliven designer Kelli Ford's Southhampton family vacation home.

PAGES 118-119 Using existing delft tile as the starting point for her Southampton living room's design, Kelli Ford and her design partner (and sister) Kirsten Fitzgibbons introduced complementary fabrics, such as the ikat prints used for chairs and pillows and the sofa's solid purple upholstery. "We let the tiles tell us what colors to use," Ford says.

LEFT The dining chairs' taupe-and-white gingham fabric contrasts with the room's cerulean walls. By leaving the windows bare, the designers ensured an unimpeded view of Shinnecock Bay's natural landscape. Ford says that her Hamptons house is "sited so beautifully, in one of the best spots for watching the setting sun."

ABOVE Inheriting the kitchen's checkerboard-tiled walls and a rack of faience plates, Ford and her sister felt little need to alter the blue-and-white space given their preference for the classic color combination. "Anyone who knows our work would understand," Fitzgibbons says.

ABOVE Purple walls add color dimension to a guest bedroom, where an exuberantly patterned Svenskt Tenn cotton fabric dresses the window and beds.

RIGHT The upstairs landing is lavished in polished mahogany paneling like a luxury ship interior—the only sailing reference in the entire house.

Tile

Cool to the touch and water resistant, decorative ceramic tile is a particularly useful material in warm and damp environments—so it fits right into waterside abodes. The geometrically patterned, glazed ceramic tile used today has a rich history dating to 13th-century Spain and Portugal, where handmade patterned tiles called azulejos were used as wall finishes throughout the region, including at the Alhambra palace in Granada. Typically polychromatic or designed in shades of blue and white, azulejos inspired similar styles of tile in both Morocco and the Netherlands, where the distinctive blue-and-white tiles are known as delft.

Today, glazed decorative tiles remain a much-loved wall material—especially in coastal homes. But their use varies. Kelli Ford's house proves true the adage that you can never have too much of a good thing, while some designers opt to employ a "little goes a long way," using tiles as an accent rather than a defining feature. To enliven the white walls of a Sea Island, Georgia, beach house, designer Sara Gilbane lined fireplace surrounds in geometrically styled tile, adding just enough zing without overwhelming the room in color or pattern (page 139). Likewise, designer Beth Webb used a neutral-colored Moroccan tile backsplash to quietly punctuate the kitchen in her clients' tranquil Costa Rican house (page 101).

Even patternless glazed tile can make a state-ment, particularly if its finish dazzles. In Veronica Swanson Beard's Nantucket kitchen (page 151), the homeowner and her designer gave the backsplash some "rhythm" with shimmering pearlescent-glazed Moroccan tile, a material every bit as alluring as the patterned variety.

ABOVE Ceramic jars, an inlaid table, and a lush bunch of hydrangea amplify the living room's blue-and-white color theme, particularly its tiled walls.

BELOW Deep-blue tile and accent trim transform the primary bathroom into a hammam, where soaking in the tub means gazing out onto the natural landscape. A tole palm tree adds a touch of whimsy.

~~~~~~

GLOBAL FUSION

Traditional Provençal details lend French flair to
a Mark D. Sikes–designed home in Southern California.

LEFT Owned by clothing designer Karen Kane and her husband, this Pacific Palisades house is awash in blue and white, starting with the entry's Portuguese-tile stair treads. "The entry looks right into the dining room, which looks into the living room, which looks into the breakfast room," designer Mark D. Sikes says. "Because everything's exposed, I used color to keep it cohesive."

RIGHT In the homeowner's office, cream-colored walls, a rattan sofa, and a woven carpet are enlivened by blue-and-white-striped fabric by Schumacher.

LEFT French Provençal dining chairs complement the kitchen's Francophile details, like a terra-cotta tile floor and casual blue-and-white fabrics. The tole ceiling light is by Charles Edwards.

ABOVE The kitchen radiates aged warmth, a result of creamy white cabinetry, vintage-inspired light fixtures, and oil-rubbed bronze hardware. "We made a 40-year-old house feel like it was built 100 years ago," Sikes says.

RIGHT The dining room wears three different Brunschwig & Fils paisley fabrics on its walls and windows, while the dining chairs are bedecked in checks. "You get the best balance by mixing one 'hero' print, a couple of solids, a geometric, and then maybe a delicate print," Sikes says.

LEFT Rattan armchairs, simple matchstick blinds, and a rug that resembles the sea speak to the home's Southern California coastal setting.

LEFT The cohesive palette of blue and white brings together the guest bedroom's eclectic mix of prints, including Persian flowers and ikats. The rush bench is a nod to Provençal style.

LEFT A vintage wicker desk serves as a bedside table. Blue accents include a geometric-patterned fabric that was used for upholstery and draperies, framed botanicals, and a four-poster bed.

LEFT Sikes was inspired by Monet's kitchen in Giverny, resulting in the pool bath's walls being lined in similar tilework. Kane feels kinship with her designer. "Mark and I, we try to create beauty in people's lives. Whether it's your backyard, your house, or the clothes you wear, it's important to put something pretty in front of your face."

"Blue has the most beautiful range, from robin's egg to cobalt, from sky to indigo."

—DESIGNER MARK D. SIKES

CHAPTER FIVE

Lasting Legacies

COASTAL LIVING IS STEEPED IN WATERSIDE CUSTOMS, like adorning a home's interiors with nods to shipbuilding and seafaring or cladding its exterior in hardy shingles, an established practice in areas where the briny air is especially punishing. Whether a house embodies a locale's maritime heritage or nods to seafaring lore, embracing time-honored coastal traditions enhances the pleasure of dwelling near the water.

Nantucket's design vernacular famously reflects its whaling past, with 19th-century woolies and shadowbox ships still considered essential decor for homes on the island. In Veronica Swanson Beard's home, Beard and designer Michelle Holland pair nautically themed antiques with a rich, cozy palette, imbuing the young structure with a sense of history. Designer Gary McBournie and Bill Richards took a different tack for their Nantucket residence. White walls and trim enriched with blue and red accents create an almost modern backdrop for their seafaring decor.

Along the Connecticut River, designer Cathy Kincaid combined the original structure of an 18th-century ship captain's cottage with a 1980s addition, deploying a nuanced palette of browns, grays, and forest green and embracing snug spaces like daybeds and window seats that felt harmonious with the home's original scale.

Even relatively young resort communities have their own hallowed traditions. When designer Sara Gilbane and architect Thad Truett embarked on building a new vacation home on Sea Island, Georgia, they sought to channel the resort's 1920s roots, when Mediterranean-style architecture was the rage. A pink exterior and terra-cotta tile roof may appear Jazz Age, but inside, the house is thoroughly 21st century. A similar reverence for the past influenced Veere Grenney's restoration of a 1970s villa on the island of Mustique, where owning a home dating to the island's '70s-era heyday is a badge of honor. "If you knew it in the old days, you would think very little has changed"—a sentiment that could apply to many waterside homes.

JAZZ AGE REVIVAL

A grand yet functional coastal getaway
design by Sara Gilbane and architect Thad Truett pays
homage to Sea Island, Georgia's dazzling past.

LEFT The Sea Island home's architect, Thad Truett, says the rosy-hued abode was designed to "carry on the spirit of the original Mediterranean-style house" that once stood on the property. The home's interior architecture also embraces the island resort's 1920s roots with its grand fireplaces and coffered pecky cypress ceilings, which designer Sara Gilbane likens to "a walk in the woods."

RIGHT Elegant furniture elevates the tone of the main salon, while a Moroccan tilework fireplace surround adds a "wow factor," according to Gilbane. The room's teal, green, and saffron yellow palette—an unusual choice for a beach house—befits the ocean lapping the Sea Island coastline, which the designer describes as "not a tropical turquoise but a deep, murky blue-green."

LEFT Gilbane chose the loggia's outdoor furniture by McKinnon and Harris for its heft. "Being this close to the ocean, you don't want flying furniture," she says.

RIGHT Guests can play backgammon in one corner of the main salon, where a banquette and a games table stand at the ready. The mirrored niche and painted palm tree accents add some seaside fun to the space. The designer refers to the salon as "a cocktail party of furniture."

"The clients opted to build something that could fit them and their family and friends forever."

—DESIGNER SARA GILBANE

RIGHT The kitchen's beamed ceiling was inspired by the work of architect Addison Mizner, who designed Sea Island's fabled resort, the Cloister, in the late 1920s. Classic blue-and-white accents include a tiled backsplash, ceramic lamps, and a snappy patterned sofa.

LEFT The butler's pantry is awash in oceanic hues, courtesy of deep sea-green-tiled walls. An octagonal leaded glass window, designed by Truett, filters light into the jewel-box space.

RIGHT A banquette dressed in fabrics by Penny Morrison summons guests for drinks in the third-floor tower bar. An extravagantly coffered ceiling speaks to the Moorish influence on the island's much-loved Mediterranean Revival style.

LIVING HISTORY

Fashion designer Veronica Swanson Beard imbues a Nantucket cottage that's steeped in tradition with poise, warmth, and nautical nods tied to the island's bygone days.

LEFT A stenciled ceiling and beadboard walls, coupled with earthy tones, give the home's entry the look and feel of an old Nantucket house. Designer Michelle Holland says that despite the island's polished resort surface, "there's still an element of the creative survivor soul that made Nantucket what it is. This is what Veronica fell in love with."

RIGHT Wicker chairs are a classic touch on the dining porch, where the table is set with additional woven details, such as placemats and napkins.

RIGHT The cozy study is decorated with an eclectic mix that includes a pair of vintage Lucite and bamboo chairs and traditional coastal artwork, like framed shadowbox ships and Alfred Birdsey watercolors.

"I envisioned us here in the off-season,
and I wanted our place to feel cozy and layered."

—HOMEOWNER VERONICA SWANSON BEARD

LEFT A gate-leg dining table and custom Windsor chairs hark back to the 18th and 19th centuries, when both furniture styles would likely have been found in homes on the island.

RIGHT The kitchen's checkerboard floor, by decorative artist Kevin Paulsen, extends throughout most of the first level, introducing an aged-looking patina to the house. Pearlescent Moroccan-tiled walls and the cooktop's slate backsplash are joined by rustic wooden counters.

"There's still an element of the creative survivor soul
that made Nantucket what it is."

—INTERIOR DESIGNER MICHELLE HOLLAND

RIGHT Paulsen also created the hand-printed muslin wallpaper that animates many of the first-floor walls and double-height stairwell, seen here. Partnered with woodwork that was made to look old by rubbing, painting, and glazing it, the wallpaper gives an aged impression.

BELOW Geometric-print wallpaper by Galbraith & Paul envelops another son's room, where turquoise-colored coverlets and whale prints echo the nearby ocean.

ABOVE A son's bedroom pairs seagrass wallpaper by Maya Romanoff with aquatic blue painted trim and ceiling, creating a suitable backdrop for the ship paintings that hang on the wall.

RIGHT A damask-print fabric was used for the drapery, window shades, and bed pelmet in the primary bedroom. A pair of wing chairs, covered in a golden fabric, and an amber-colored bell-jar lantern lend added warmth to the cosseting space.

LEFT On the south porch, vintage rattan chairs sport cushions covered in a Jane Shelton fabric. Radiant Rose hollyhock and Invincibelle Spirit II hydrangea frame the house.

LEFT A sage-colored wallpaper by Sister Parish makes the vaulted guest bedroom feel cozy. The bell-jar lantern and patchwork quilt are classic American designs that provide a colorful decorative connection to the past.

Nautical Details

For centuries, seafaring has been at the heart of a coastal lifestyle. For some, it is a livelihood; for others, an exhilarating recreation. Either way, sailing and the lore associated with it remains a popular source of inspiration when decorating waterside houses.

In traditionally styled coastal homes, nautical-related antiques are popular, such as ship paintings, shell-encrusted boxes, sailors' valentines, and 19th-century woolies, which are scenes of ships that were embroidered by sailors using wool thread. Describing herself as a collector, Veronica Swanson Beard hung woolies and ship shadowboxes on the walls of her Nantucket home, paying homage to the island's maritime history—a reference that extends to a bedroom, where classic brass railings attached to a bunk bed call to mind a ship's sleeping quarters.

Fascination with ships sometimes influences a room's interior architecture. In Kelli Ford's Southampton beach house, the upstairs hallway is sheathed in polished mahogany paneling, emulating the look of a ship's interior—or possibly the deck of a vintage Chris-Craft boat (page 123). And it's not just beach homes that have license to indulge in nautical accents. For the inn she refurbished on Lake Michigan, designer Summer Thornton lined a small bar in a collage of ship paintings, a design conducive to conviviality, and perhaps the singing of a sea shanty or two (page 77).

LEFT Brass railings and ticking-stripe bedding are reminiscent of a ship's sleeping quarters.

ABOVE A pleated skirt wrapped around the sink and 1920s-inspired wall sconces by Jamb supply the powder room with vintage-style charm.

CARIBBEAN CHIC

London decorator Veere Grenney restores a '70s-era
landmark home on Mustique to its former glory.

LEFT Designed in the
1970s by Englishman
Oliver Messel, a onetime
set decorator responsible
for many of the island's
most prominent houses,
the villa has a lily pond
on one side and the
Caribbean Sea on the other.
"If you think of Mustique,
you think of the 1970s,"
Grenney says.

RIGHT The breezy
dining room epitomizes
the easygoing spirit
and carefree decor that
defines the entire
house. "It's all wicker, it's
all treillage, and it's all
very simple detailing—
nothing sophisticated,"
Grenney says.

PAGES 160-161 Despite
overhauling the entirety
of this Mustique house,
Veere Grenney preserved
its original unpretentious
personality by using
rattan and wicker furniture
and humble finishes,
such as the living room's
woven natural rug. "When
the houses here were
built, they were absolutely
charming, but most
had no real luxury per se.
They were slightly
old-fashioned and very
English," Grenney says.

RIGHT Grenney hewed to
mostly white furnishings,
including a plaster palm
floor lamp and a pool table
painted white in the
billiards room.

LEFT Trellis-lined walls, a Soane Britain wicker lamp, and a mostly white color scheme give a guest bedroom a weightless appearance.

LEFT Some of the living room's seating has Caribbean-blue cushions, a nod to the room's spectacular sea views.

LEFT Striped banding on an armchair and ottomans is the only note of pattern in the primary bedroom. The bed's linen netting protects sleepers from pesky mosquitos.

HISTORICAL ADAPTATION

Cathy Kincaid tailors an 18th-century ferry captain's cottage on the Connecticut River for the 21st century with layers of cozy prints and an earthy palette.

LEFT Located on the banks of the Connecticut River, seen here through an archway, a 1748 ferryman's cottage has expanded over time to include an outsize 1980s-built wing and, more recently, a modestly proportioned addition that better resembles the original structure. "When people visit, they can't tell where the old part ends and the new begins," says the current homeowner, who spends her summers here.

RIGHT Located in the original part of the house, the dining room's seating nook is bedecked in Sister Parish fabrics, used for drapery and upholstery. The walls were painted a cozy shade: French Gray by Farrow & Ball.

LEFT Known for her elegant, and highly livable, style of decorating, Cathy Kincaid devised what has become the homeowner's favorite spot: a French-blue window seat in the family room that overlooks the river. "It epitomizes the best of the house: the views, the charm, the scale, the comfort. It's divine and totally unplugged," the owner says.

RIGHT The butler's pantry was given historically accurate flair with wallpaper by Adelphi Paper Hangings. The pattern dates to the 18th century.

"We nodded to that cozy New England look."

—DESIGNER CATHY KINCAID

ABOVE The entry hall, a newly constructed addition designed to tie together the original part of the house and the 1980s addition, is finished in chestnut flooring and painted wall paneling, giving the space an aged appearance. The painted screen is an early 19th-century Provençal piece.

RIGHT Architect Brooke Girty used historically proportioned panes of glass in the entry hall's giant window, making the addition compatible with the original house.

LEFT The beamed primary bedroom charms with its traditional decor, particularly a bed canopy fashioned from a fabric whose pattern resembles Colonial-era stenciling. Kincaid says that draperies and canopies "can make a room feel softer and more layered and help distract from awkward architectural angles."

RIGHT An antique birdhouse inspired the design of the pool pavilion. Inside, a wraparound banquette provides a comfortable perch for entertaining or simply relaxing. "Everywhere else, I feel like I should stay busy. But here, I don't feel guilty curling up with a book," the homeowner says.

RIGHT A paisley print fabric, which Kincaid used for drapery, headboards, and bed skirts, headlines a guest bedroom. The designer thought of every necessity, including a luggage rack from Colefax and Fowler.

ABOVE Protected by a vine-covered pergola, a stone terrace provides the homeowners with a spot for outdoor dining. The home's landscape was designed to be increasingly wild the farther away one is from the house.

~~~~~~~~

RIGHT The owners appreciate the home's location on the river, which puts them—and their motor yacht—in close proximity to the Hamptons. "It's a great jumping-off point," the owner says.

SAILOR MADE

Gary McBournie and Bill Richards's
crisp and casual Nantucket home
embraces the island's nautical heritage.

LEFT The homeowners also collect the island's famed woven baskets and antique sailors' valentines, seen to the right of the living room. A type of shell art believed to have originated in Barbados, sailors' valentines were souvenirs traditionally brought home by returning sailors in the 19th century.

RIGHT A rope banister adds a snappy nautical detail to the stairwell, as do an assortment of ship paintings—a curated mix that Richards says enhances the home's maritime theme. "When we do a home, it's a collection of things, and it never looks like we just went to a design center and picked out as many objects aswe could."

PAGES 180-181 A formerly dark boathouse was transformed into a bright environment for the homeowners' collection of quintessentially Nantucket pieces, such as the living room's antique model ships.

> "We really committed to doing something that celebrated Nantucket and its artisans."
>
> —HOMEOWNER BILL RICHARDS

LEFT The dining room, with formal chairs surrounding a whitewashed table, is where the homeowners frequently entertain. A vintage wooden anchor and a ship painting speak to the area's history. "One of the things that is distinctive about us is how we put different things together," Richards says.

RIGHT An antique hutch holds a bevy of antique blue-and-white china.

RIGHT Like much of the house, the guest bedroom is awash in a sea of blue and white. Striped drapery fabric by John Robshaw and bed linens embroidered with a ropelike design give the space a shipshape appearance.

RIGHT Arranged in the
outdoor living room,
vintage bamboo
seating looks crisp with
cushions covered in
a blue Perennials fabric
and pillows designed
by McBournie.

CHAPTER SIX

Personal Nature

A COASTAL LIFESTYLE CAN BE AS FREE and uninhibited as an incoming ocean tide. Likewise, boundlessness spills over into waterside design, where the freedom to express oneself can produce dwellings as unique as seashells swept onshore.

Some houses are so ingrained with their owners' personality that they become bastions of individuality. When interior designer and antiques dealer Lou Marotta and his partner decamped from New York City to the sunny climes of West Palm Beach, they found a house that appealed to Marotta's sophisticated sense of whimsy—a 1926 Mediterranean Revival residence. "Moorish architecture is all about fantasy," says Marotta, who commissioned a fanciful black-and-white mural of a gazebo for the reception hall. He also gave pride of place to furniture rarely seen in beach houses, such as a table designed by Albert Hadley.

But for a house blessed with marshland views from Sea Island, Georgia, it was a magpie mix of pieces diligently assembled by the homeowner that prompted designer Ellen Kavanaugh's audacious take on marsh-side decor: a brass handbag, a collection of seashells, and a vintage book about the film *Jaws*. "We immediately got a sense of what the house needed to look like: a bit of throwback '70s and '80s glam mixed with this very natural beach house that needed to be filled with casual materials and textures," Kavanaugh says. An iridescent-tile kitchen backsplash and disco-era furniture are unexpected additions to an otherwise natural environment.

Even boat interiors can be open to interpretation. Tasked with outfitting a couple's racing yacht, designer Ken Fulk immersed himself in nautical design, learning the ropes by joining a racing crew. Although functionality drove much of the yacht's interior design, Fulk personalized it through flourishes that speak to his client's time spent living in Hawaii. Hand-carved doors and embossed leather upholstery both bear the symbolic markings of indigenous Hawaiian design. "Patterns and fabrics act as storytelling devices," Fulk says. So, too, do many homes.

GOLDEN ISLES GLAMOUR

Ellen Kavanaugh brings throwback shimmer and shine
to a house on the marshes of Sea Island, Georgia.

LEFT Brass accents, including flush mounts from CB2 and a geometric-patterned wallpaper by Phillip Jeffries, glamorize the bar.

PAGES 192-193 Ellen Kavanaugh welcomed the opportunity to decorate her friend's marsh-side home. "I spent a lot of time in marsh-front settings when growing up, so getting to work on Sea Island is very nostalgic to me," she says. Equally nostalgic is the home's 1970s vibe, evident in the living room's vintage furnishings, which include pieces by Milo Baughman and Warren Platner.

LEFT Throughout the home, bold accents are tempered by natural finishes, such as cypress wood, and paint colors, like Benjamin Moore's Maidenhair Fern shade, which was used on shutters.

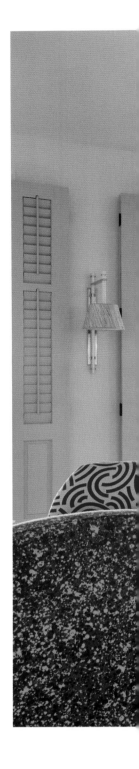

LEFT The kitchen's backsplash, made from the Paris Ceramics iridescent tile that Kavanaugh had long dreamed of using, glistens like shells. The designer describes the cabinetry's hushed pink hue as "super-soft, barely there blush."

RIGHT The powder room is enveloped in Osborne and Little's crane-patterned wallpaper, which speaks to the rich wildlife that inhabits the area. A vintage brass and acrylic mirror adds some '70s-inspired flair.

~~~~~~~~~~

ABOVE The center of the spacious living room is set for casual dining around a Parsons-style table. Low, unobtrusive seating, including two pairs of acrylic and leather benches and vintage reed stools covered in bouclé, helps the room maintain its airy feeling.

"This house touches on all these childhood memories we've shared over the years, plus the '70s glam we saw from our parents."

—DESIGNER ELLEN KAVANAUGH

LEFT Vintage lighting and a tropical-print fabric by Manuel Canovas give the primary bedroom a retro-coastal vibe reminiscent of a glamorous old beach resort.

ABOVE The bedroom's tropical print upholstery is repeated in the closet, this time appearing on leafy wallpaper amplified by green trim. Conch-shell pink walls create a flattering environment in the bathroom.

RIGHT The poolside cabana embraces its coastal location with warm, nacreous tile and a pair of shell-backed chairs.

ABOVE The woven seagrass rug and textured wallcovering in the family room exude a casual Low Country feel that complements the home's marshland setting. Vintage chairs and a sofa by Coup Studio wear fabric seemingly made for the home's setting: Shell Grotto by Fermoie.

GREAT ESCAPE

At the hands of Ken Fulk, a racing yacht charts its own course
with Hawaiian-inspired accents and luxurious details.

ABOVE Named *Halekai*, meaning "home on the sea," the yacht sports a claret-and-saffron-striped hull—colors borrowed from the interior color scheme.

LEFT The main saloon offers comfort and amusement with a wall-length sofa covered in an Hermès fabric and a games table that flips over to become a coffee table. Fulk designed the interiors so that everything can be secured when the boat is racing.

PAGES 202-203 Designer Ken Fulk heaped the yacht's sundeck with an array of cushions, some of which are covered in a yucca-print fabric by Holly Hunt. "Everyone wants to pile on," he says.

RIGHT The upper dining saloon's banquette features a Cubist-patterned fabric, which Fulk had trimmed in leather embossed with Hawaiian symbols. The woodwork is teak, a material often used for boat interiors.

LEFT In the owners' berth, the headboard quilt and a shadowbox with a miniature scarlet feather circlet are Hawaiian inspired. The shelving's metal rods have dual roles, serving as escape ladders and as a means of keeping items on the shelves secure.

ABOVE Like the rest of the yacht, the guest bathroom is luxuriously appointed, with a honey-onyx sink backsplash and wall sconces that Fulk says are "low profile but high style."

ABOVE Evening cocktails are mixed at the teak-and-raffia-lined bar, where a pair of bar stools are trimmed in pink leather. Fulk designed the boat's cabinetry and built-ins with eased corners, a safety feature that is especially important on the high seas.

RIGHT The cockpit has both raw and varnished teak finishes, a combination that inspired the mix of matte and glossy surfaces used in the interiors. Cushions provide perches from which to survey the aquatic landscape.

"A yacht like this is a fiercely athletic machine that also has to be able to offer elegant, Gatsby-like entertaining. All the craftsmanship is driven by purpose."

—DESIGNER KEN FULK

BLITHE SPIRIT

Lou Marotta makes a West Palm Beach house his own with an eclectic mix
of treasures and an enviable furniture collection.

LEFT Surrounded by lush tropical landscaping, the outdoor dining terrace of Lou Marotta's West Palm Beach home faces Lake Worth Lagoon. A 1930s Italian table presents a note of grandeur to the otherwise casual space.

RIGHT A casual attitude prevails in the sunroom, where a set of custom swivel chairs are covered in a brown-and-white ikat print and a carved-concrete coffee table from the 1920s is joined by a contemporary ceiling pendant. "The best way to make things work together is serious editing, which is my specialty," Marotta says.

LEFT "Because of all the moisture in the air, saturated colors seem to sparkle here. Even simple whites that would normally fall flat become so lively," Marotta says. The home's vivacious white-and-coral living room proves that theory true. A round plaster table designed by Albert Hadley stands near an ottoman formerly owned by Sister Parish.

RIGHT The home's reception hall, which doubles as a dining room, features a delightful black-and-white gazebo-design mural that is accented by vines and passionflowers. The dining table and chairs are vintage French pieces, a sampling of Marotta's lauded collection of eclectic antique and vintage furnishings.

Outdoor Living Spaces

Watery landscapes have a way of luring people out of their homes, beckoning them to spend as much time outdoors as possible. That draw is especially strong in warm climates, where a home's outdoor living space can see as much—or more—year-round activity as its interior environment.

Their styles might vary, but outdoor spaces often have one thing in common: design continuity, meaning that they tend to be furnished similarly to the home's interior. When Lou Marotta fashioned his home's alfresco dining room, he designated an antique Baroque-style table as the centerpiece, an operatic design gesture akin to those inside the house.

Covered outdoor spaces invite frequent use even in inclement weather. Partially protected by a coffered ceiling, the spacious loggia of a coastal Georgia retreat provided designer Sara Gilbane with the opportunity to create multiple living spaces, including both a dining setup and a seating area enhanced by a fireplace—a bonus when the weather is chilly (page 140).

Some of the most enjoyable outdoor living spaces, however, are unconnected to a main house, a distance that lets them become full-fledged destinations. At her clients' Connecticut River property, designer Cathy Kincaid fashioned a luxurious spot for drinks or afternoon tea within a fanciful pool pavilion (page 175). Replete with upholstered banquettes, light fixtures, and even art pieces on the wall, the elegant space acts as a retreat within a retreat—the purpose of any good outdoor space.

RIGHT A pair of Greek philosophers, in the form of carved stone, stands watch over the pool. The teak lounge chairs are outfitted with outdoor fabric cushions.

index

NOTE: **Page references of photos indicate locations of captions.**

photography credits

M.K. Sadler: Cover, 7, 80–87
Getty Images 1, 11, 41, 79, 105, 137, 191
Ngoc Minh Ngo 2–3, 146–159
Angie Silvy 4, 202–211
Pascal Chevallier 8, 106–117
Erin Little 12–21
Nick Mele 22–31
Pieter Estersohn 32–39
Thomas Loof 42–55
Dylan Thomas 56–65
Annie Schlechter 66–77, 180–189
Richard Powers 88–95
Laura Resen 96–103, back cover
Melanie Acevedo 118–125
Amy Neunsinger 126–135
Zach & Buj 138–145
David Oliver 160–167
Tria Giovan 168–179
Carmel Brantley 192–201
Bjorn Wallander 212–219
Erica George Dines 223 (top)
Brian Woodcock 223 (bottom)

JENNIFER BOLES is a writer and cultural historian and has been featured in numerous publications, including *The New York Times, Town & Country,* and *Wall Street Journal.* She is a contributing writer to many magazines and the author of *Inspired Design: The 100 Most Important Interior Designers of the Past 100 Years.*

STEELE THOMAS MARCOUX is the editor of VERANDA and a veteran of the design publishing industry, having served in senior editorial roles at *Country Living, Coastal Living,* and *Southern Living.* She is a member of the board of directors of the Alabama School of Fine Arts in Birmingham, where she lives with her husband, two sons, and two dogs.